Safe Movi and Handl Made Easy

Contents

Edition 1.1

Tel: 0845 644 3305
www.qualsafe.com

Introduction to Manual Handling

Definition of Manual Handling

Manual handling is any activity that includes lifting or putting down, pulling or pushing, carrying, supporting or moving an object, person or animal using the hand or any other part of the body. Many people make the assumption that manual handling only applies when items are lifted, but it could be ANY movement of an object.

Common Causes of Workplace Injuries

The most common causes for manual handling injuries vary depending on the type of injury sustained. However, some of the most common causes are:

- Poor posture.
- Heavy lifting or using excessive force.
- Excessive repetition of a task.
- Lack of time to recover from the task.
- Twisting and stooping activities.
- Pushing or pulling loads over a prolonged distance.
- Reaching or lifting away from the body.
- Standing or sitting in a static position without regular changes in posture.
- Person's own susceptibility to injury.

About a third of all workplace accidents reported to the HSE are as a direct result of handling, lifting or carrying.

The Cost of Manual Handling Injuries

Manual handling injuries can have a serious effect on employers and employees.

Business costs

- Legal advice and insurance costs.
- Legal action, possibly including compensation.
- Sick pay.
- Lost production and sales.
- Equipment and stock losses or damages.
- Time and money spent on investigation and improvements.
- Recruitment and cost of cover/replacement staff.

But these can fade into insignificance when weighed against the human costs.

Human costs

- Pain and suffering.
- Disability, possibly long-term.
- Potential loss of life.
- Health care and rehabilitation.
- Loss of earnings.
- Emotional and financial burden on family.

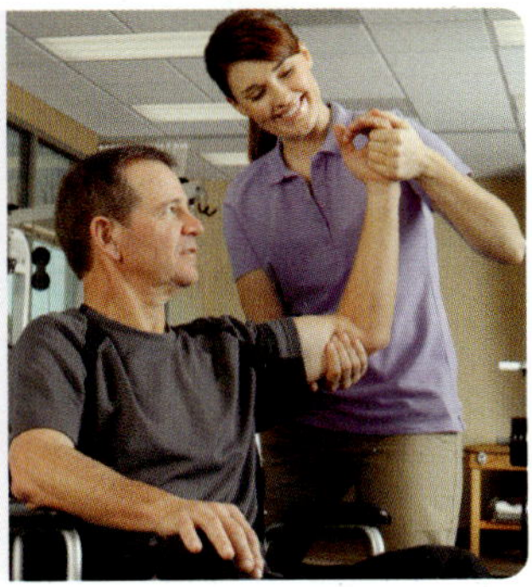

Risk Controls

When you weigh up the human and business costs that manual handling injuries cause, it is clear that avoiding injury in the first place is to everyone's advantage.

The employer and employee need to consider:

The Hazard – things that have potential to do harm.

The Risk – the likelihood of the hazard actually doing harm.

Control Measures – actions or procedures put into place to reduce risk to an acceptable level.

Manual Handling and the Law

There are a number of laws relating to manual handling that cover the responsibilities of employers, employees and the self employed.

Health and Safety at Work etc. Act (1974)

The Health and Safety at Work Act came into force in 1974 and covers everyone at work *(apart from persons attending domestic premises)*. The Act makes it clear that everyone has a part to play in health and safety and aims to encourage high standards and prevent people coming to harm while in their working environment. The responsibilities of various parties under the Act are detailed below:

Employers

The Act places a 'duty of care' on employers to introduce good health and safety practices and provides a framework for health and safety regulations. They must ensure the health, safety and welfare of employees, visitors and the public by providing:

- A written Health and Safety Policy *(if they employ 5 or more people).*
- Safe equipment and machinery.
- Safe systems of work.
- Information, instruction, supervision and training.
- A safe working environment.
- Adequate welfare facilities.

Employees

Under the Health and Safety at Work Act all employees have a duty to:

- Act in a way that does not put themselves or others at risk.
- Co-operate with their employer on any health and safety matters.

Self-Employed

The self employed share many of the same duties of employers and must ensure that their work does not endanger themselves or others and should inform people of hazards e.g. by putting up signs to alert others to potential dangers.

Occupiers of Buildings

Persons in control of buildings have duties to people who are not employed by them but work at or visit the premises e.g. customers, contractors, visitors, etc.

Designers, Manufacturers and Installers

Equipment and articles must be designed, constructed and tested to ensure they will work safely and any substances used in their manufacture must be safe. Adequate information on the safe use of the equipment must be provided.

Manual Handling Operations Regulations (1992)

This regulation is specific to manual handling responsibilities and outlines a clear 'Hierarchy of Control' – AVOID, ASSESS, REDUCE, REVIEW *(for more details on 'Hierarchy of Control' see Risk Assessment chapter on page 17).*

Employer's responsibilities

Where possible, employers should **AVOID** the need for employees to perform any manual handling tasks at work which could result in them being injured.

Where it is not possible to avoid manual handling tasks at work they must:

- Make a suitable **ASSESS**ment of the task to be undertaken.
- Take steps to **REDUCE** the risk of injury.
- Inform employees of the weight of the load.
- **REVIEW** procedures if there has been a significant change to the manual handling operation or task.

Employee's responsibilities

All employees have a duty to:

- Follow safe systems provided.

Management of Health and Safety at Work Regulations (1999)

Employer's responsibilities

Besides carrying out a risk assessment, employers also need to:

- Make arrangements for implementing the health and safety measures identified as necessary by the risk assessment.
- Appoint a competent person *(someone who has sufficient training, experience or knowledge to enable them to assist the employer in complying with Health and Safety legislation)*.
- Set up emergency procedures.
- Provide clear information and training to employees.
- Pay particular attention to high risk groups such as under 18s and new or expectant mothers.
- Work together with other employers sharing the same workplace.

Employee's responsibilities

- Use any equipment and safety device given to them by their employer in the way in which they were trained.
- Advise an employer if they have noticed any risk or danger in the workplace.

Reporting of Injuries, Diseases and Dangerous Occurrences Regulations (1995) – (RIDDOR)

RIDDOR requires employers *(including the self employed)* or those in control of premises to report any work related deaths, major injuries, cases of disease or near miss incidents involving their employees immediately to the HSE.

Injuries that have occurred at work which mean the worker is absent or unable to do their work for more than 7 days need to be reported within 15 days of the accident occurring.

By Law, employers must also keep a record of all injuries which result in workers being unable to work for over 3 days *(an accident book entry is acceptable)*. However, it is good practice to record all accidents and near misses.

Provision and Use of Work Equipment Regulations (PUWER 1998)

Lifting Operations and Lifting Equipment Regulations (LOLER 1998)

These regulations specifically cover equipment and are discussed in more detail in the chapter on Manual Handling Equipment on page 34.

The courts can imprison those found guilty for up to 2 years.

Penalties and Enforcement

The Health and Safety Executive *(HSE)* and Local Authority Environmental Health Departments are responsible for enforcing most health and safety law at work. In cases where advice given has not been followed or they feel there is an unacceptable level of risk, legal notices can be served. Failure to comply with a notice is a criminal offence. Substantial fines can be issued and in severe cases, the courts can imprison those found guilty for up to 2 years.

The HSE's job is to protect people from risk and subsequent injury at work. Guidance on all health and safety related topics can be found on their website – www.hse.gov.uk

The Musculoskeletal System

The musculoskeletal system is made up of two systems that work together to allow you to support and move your own body – the skeletal system *(bones and joints)* and the skeletal muscle system.

Safe manual handling should protect your whole body, but specific emphasis is put on protecting the spine as this is the most commonly injured area.

The Spine

The spine has 3 main functions:

1. **To protect the spinal cord.**
2. **To allow movement.**
3. **To support the upper body.**

There are 33 bones in the spine. These bones are called vertebrae. Ligaments hold the vertebrae together.

Between each individual bone there is a disc – these discs act as shock absorbers during activities such as running, jumping and walking.

The outer part of the disc is made of lots of layers of cartilage and the inner nucleus is a softer consistency. The discs enable the spine to flex and extend, allow smooth movement of the spine and help bond the vertebrae together.

A common injury to the spine is a slipped disc. This is where the layers of cartilage of the disc can become cracked and the inner nucleus pushes out of the crack and presses on the spinal nerve *(see diagram opposite)*.

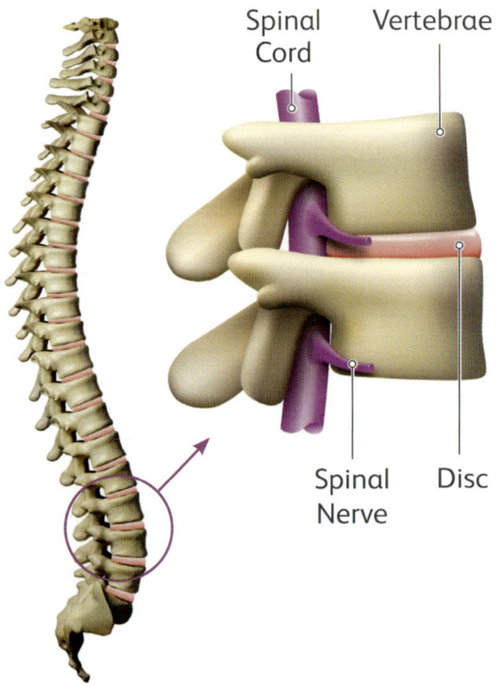

The shape of the vertebrae creates a channel. The spinal cord runs down this channel from the base of the brain. Therefore the spine plays a significant role in protecting the spinal cord. Nerves from the spinal cord branch out and leave the spine through spaces between the vertebrae.

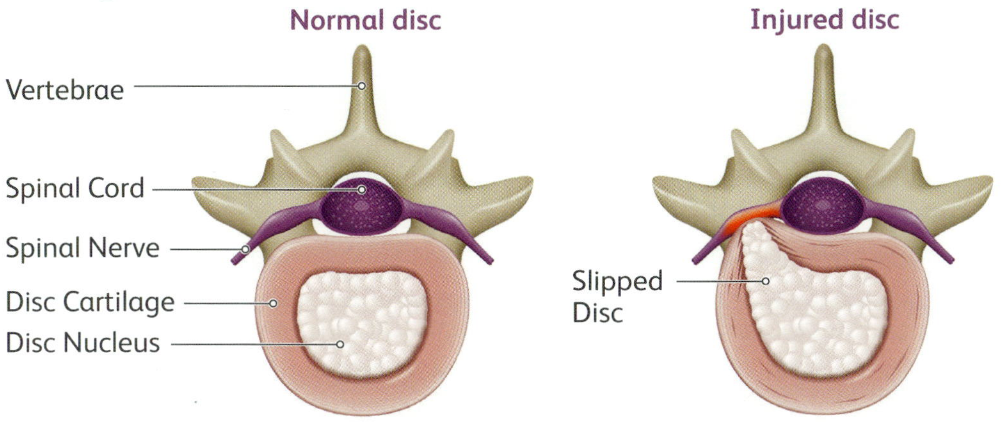

When viewed from the side, the spine has three natural curves. It is important to maintain these curves to protect the spine, optimise function and avoid damaging the spine. If the posture becomes excessive it is described as 'poor posture' *(see images below)*.

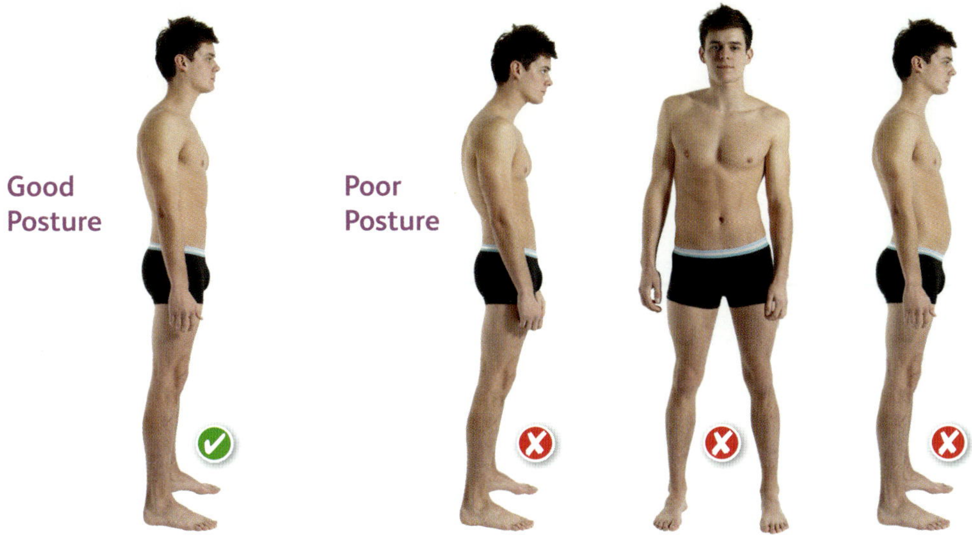

Spinal Muscles

More than 30 muscles and tendons help to provide spinal balance, stability and mobility. Muscles are attached to the vertebrae by tendons. Each separate back muscle is comparable to the size of the muscles in the hand that control the fingers, therefore it is important to note that they are not designed to do strong prolonged contractions such as lifting. Static work also tires these muscles quickly due to their size which can make you more prone to injury.

Mechanics of Movement

Understanding your own body mechanics plays a crucial role in safe manual handling.

Centre of Gravity

Every person and item has a centre of gravity. The centre of gravity is the point at which the whole weight of an object can be considered to act and therefore at which all parts of an object are balanced. When a person is standing still, their centre of gravity is located inside their body at about the level of their navel *(belly button)*. The position of the centre of gravity moves if you change your body position.

The centre of gravity can move with activity of the arms or body. The further away from the centre of gravity the activity is, the greater the pressure in the spine.

The Lever System

Your body's musculoskeletal system uses levers to produce movement so it is important to understand the basics about how levers work. All levers require a fulcrum *(pivot point)* to function. As demonstrated in the diagrams opposite, changing the distance between the fulcrum and the load can greatly affect the amount of force required to counterbalance a load.

In **figure 1** there are equal distances from the load to the fulcrum and from the fulcrum to the counterbalancing force. The counterbalancing force must be equal to the weight of the load to keep the lever balanced.

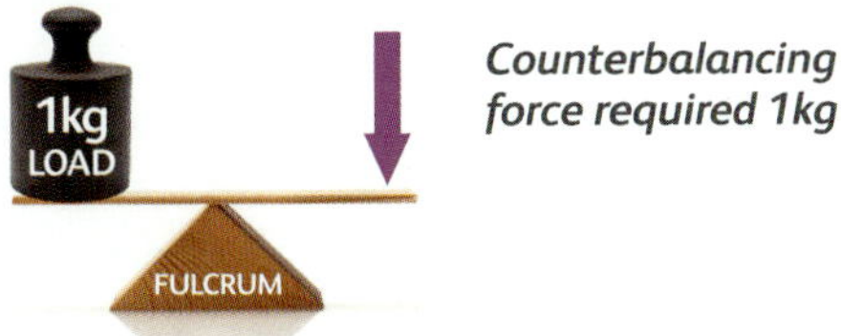

Figure 1

In **figure 2** the weight of the load and the distance between the fulcrum and the counterbalancing force is unchanged. The distance between the load and fulcrum however has increased by 5 times. Because of this extra distance, the counterbalancing force must be 5 times greater to keep the lever balanced.

Figure 2

Actually lifting a load will require a force greater than that which is needed to counterbalance it. When you lean over *(instead of bending your knees to lift an object)* you are increasing the amount of pressure on your back. Additional pressure is put on your back muscles as they are counterbalancing the weight of both the object and your upper body.

A longer lever increases the pressure on your back.

A shorter lever puts less pressure on your back.

The stability of your body when performing manual handling tasks plays an important role. You should always ensure that you have a stable base when moving objects with the centre of gravity falling within your feet. Your feet should be positioned slightly apart to give you better balance and you should bend your knees, keep your chin up and try to maintain the normal curvature of your spine. This will enable the weight to be evenly distributed from the spine to the pelvis where much **stronger leg muscles** can apply the force required to move the load. To decrease the pressure on your spine, you should hold the load close to your body. The further away from the centre of gravity the load is, the greater the pressure on the spine.

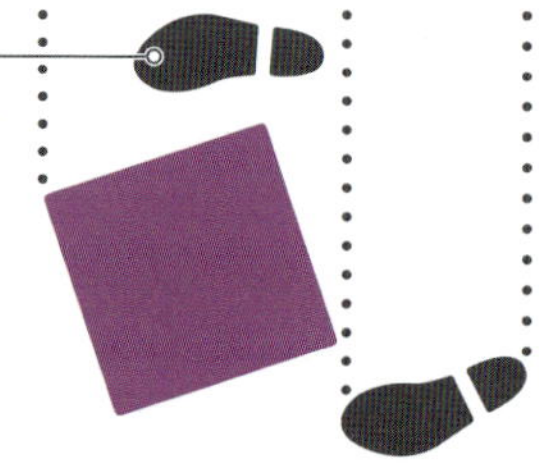

Ergonomics

Ergonomics is the science of fitting the task to the person by designing equipment and apparatus that fit well with the human body and the way that it moves. People come in all shapes and sizes so where possible work stations need to be designed with adjustable features, such as adjustable seats and work platforms, so that employees can work comfortably. Failure to do so can result in people stooping, stretching, overreaching and twisting. This can cause muscle fatigue, strain and possible long term damage or deformation.

Other factors that should be considered when risk assessing the ergonomics of work activities are:

- The degree of force that is needed to do the job.
- The environmental conditions – lighting and temperature.
- Adequacy of rest periods.
- The repetitiveness of the task.

Any machine expected to carry out repetitive motions should be regularly maintained with parts replaced as they wear out. Failure to maintain machinery may result in breakdown. People may also be expected to carry out similar repetitive tasks and suffer wear and tear. This may result in the person suffering permanent damage and being unable to work. Any activity involving high numbers of repetitions should be looked at carefully and redesigned to avoid this as much as possible.

Remedies

- Alternating tasks and work breaks to avoid repetitive strain injuries.
- Providing comfortable working temperature and adequate ventilation.
- Providing sufficient lighting and minimizing glare by glazing windows or supplying blinds.
- Vibration should be minimized.
- Mechanise the task.
- Regular health tests may be necessary and should be promoted by employers.
- Training will also help employees have a greater awareness of good practice.

Types of Manual Handling Injuries

Manual handling injuries can be due to a single event or accident or as a result of repetitive tasks or poor posture. The vast majority of manual handling injuries reported to the Health and Safety Executive are as a result of an injury to the lower back – however many other areas of the body can also be affected.

Some Common Types of Manual Handling Injuries:

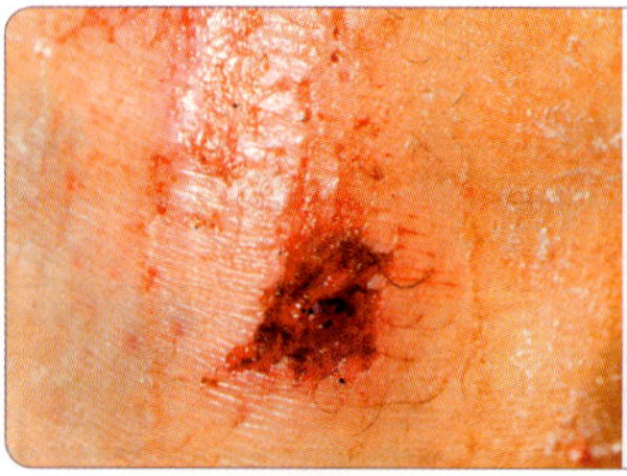

Abrasions, Cuts and Fractures

Broken skin and broken bones can occur in various parts of the body. These are often caused by a single event or accident.

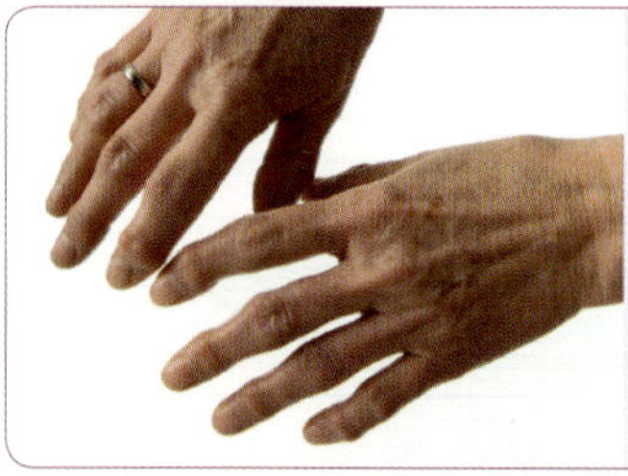

Arthritis

Inflammation of a joint. This can be caused by wear and tear due to repetitive tasks.

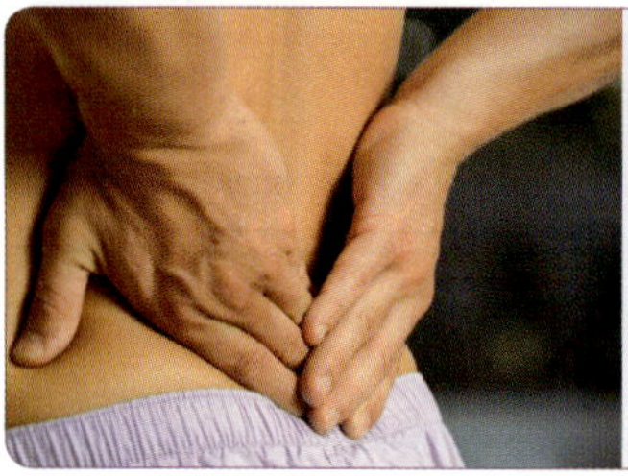

Back Pain

Pain may be as a result of muscular or nerve damage. Causes of back pain include poor static posture and heavy lifting.

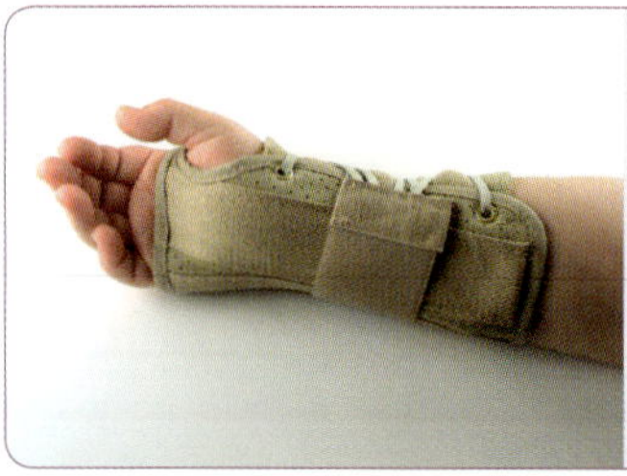

Carpal Tunnel Syndrome

A painful condition of the hands and fingers where a major nerve in the hand and wrist is compressed. Repetitive motions can cause this.

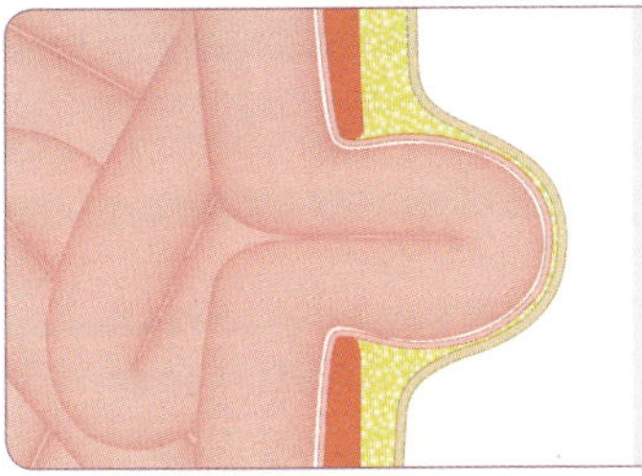

Hernia

A protrusion of tissue through a weakness in the muscle or surrounding tissue wall. This can be caused by lifting heavy objects incorrectly.

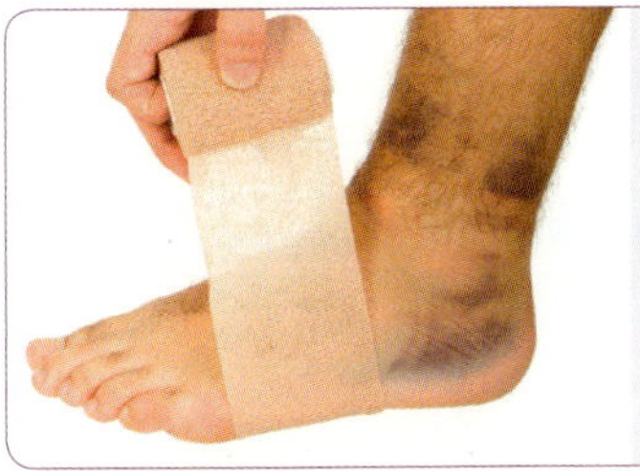

Muscle or Ligament Sprain or Strain

The muscle or ligament fibres in joints tearing as a result of overstretching *(pulled muscle)*.

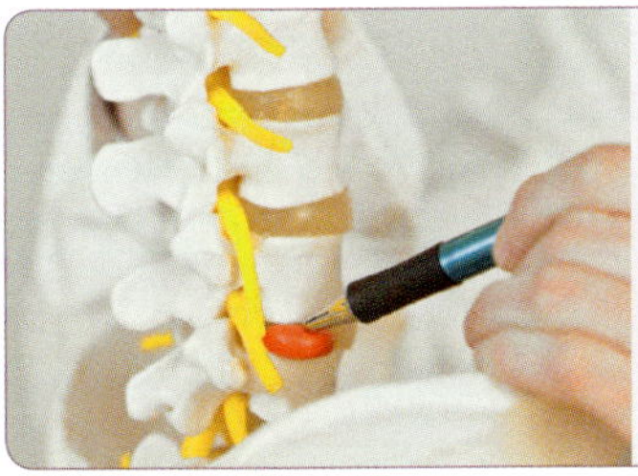

Slipped Disc

Layers of cartilage of the disc can become cracked and the inner nucleus pushes out of the crack and presses on the spinal nerve *(see diagram on page 9)*.

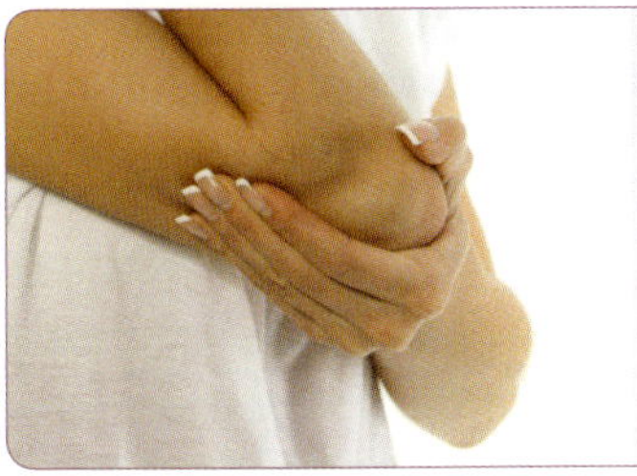

Tendonitis

Inflammation of a tendon caused by overuse.

No occupation is free from potential manual handling injuries, but some occupations are particularly susceptible to spine and lower back injuries, e.g. farmers, nurses and delivery personnel.

Other occupations are more at risk of developing injuries as a result of repetitive tasks, e.g. hairdressers and factory line workers.

You must remember that manual handling injuries can happen in your everyday life too. Therefore the safer handling principles and good posture that you apply to your work life are also relevant to your life outside of work.

Factors That Increase Risk of Harm

No individual is immune from manual handling injuries, but there are some factors that may make a person more susceptible to harm.

Task related factors that increase risk of injury:

- Heavy manual labour.
- Awkward postures.
- Vibration.
- Static work – any position held for longer than 30 seconds is considered to be a static posture.
- Bending and twisting.
- Carrying loads away from your body and away from your centre of gravity.

Personal factors that increase risk of injury:

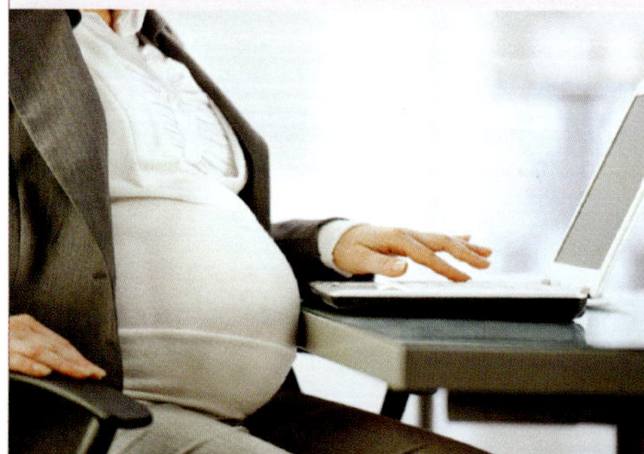

- Being overweight or unfit.
- Previous or existing injuries.
- Motherhood or pregnancy.
- Age – risk of lower back disorders increases with the number of years you have worked.
- Smoking.
- Genetic factors.

Risk Assessment

When examining the topic of risk assessment, it is first useful to understand some of the terms commonly used in risk assessment:

Reasonably Practicable – a risk/sacrifice computation made to see what safety measures are reasonable under given circumstances of cost/benefit.

Suitable and Sufficient – is the risk assessment appropriate for the given circumstances? Is it detailed enough with regard to the level of risk involved?

Competent Person – a person who has sufficient training, experience, knowledge or other relevant qualities to enable them to undertake the task or job.

Hierarchy of Control – control measures to reduce risks listed in order of priority *(Avoid, Assess, Reduce and Review – as detailed on the next page)*.

The Management of Health and Safety at Work Regulations *(1999)* requires the employer to arrange for a competent person*(s)* to carry out a detailed risk assessment. It should identify all workplace hazards, quantify the risks and introduce control measures to reduce the risk of injury or illness to the workforce. If more than five persons are employed, the assessment must be recorded. Specific risk assessments should be completed for manual handling activities.

A risk assessment is simply a careful examination of what could cause harm to people in the workplace so that you can weigh up whether you have taken enough precautions or should do more to prevent harm.

Risk assessments will help identify what could go wrong, how likely it is to happen and how serious the result could be. The employer then needs to put control measures in place to prevent the problem occurring.

Four Steps of a Manual Handling Risk Assessment

1 AVOID

Can the task be avoided?

Could a piece of equipment perform the task instead of a person?

2 ASSESS

T **Task** – Does the task involve twisting, reaching forward, carrying loads for long distances or carrying loads away from the body?

Does the task involve awkward posture, heavy manual labour or repetitive motions?

I **Individual** – Do they need Personal Protective Equipment *(PPE)*? Have they received appropriate training?

L **Load** – Consider the weight, size and stability of load.

E **Environment** – Uneven or slippery floors, poor lighting and unhelpful temperatures. Consider seasonal weather factors.

Where a manual handling task cannot be avoided remember T.I.L.E. ***(Task, Individual, Load, Environment – see pages 20–21 for more detail.)***

Decide On Who Might Be Harmed and How

It is not just the person conducting the task that may be affected, but also anyone nearby. For example, builders working on scaffolding above a public walkway may injure pedestrians if equipment or materials are dropped. If you are moving a person using manual handling techniques, the person being moved should also be considered.

Factors personal to individuals should be considered when assessing risk e.g. their level of fitness and any previous injuries. Separate risk assessments will need to be completed for employees who are more vulnerable such as pregnant workers or young inexperienced staff.

3 REDUCE

Consider the consequences of injury or harm. Could someone be seriously injured or killed? Could lots of people be affected? Is it likely to occur? If the answer is yes, then these hazards should be addressed as a priority and further controls put in place to reduce the risk to an acceptable level. Could lifting equipment be used to decrease risk? Could the way a task is organised reduce the risk of harm?

Where a manual handling task cannot be avoided and you need to reduce the level of risk remember T.I.L.E. *(Task, Individual, Load, Environment – see page 20–21 for more detail.)*

4 REVIEW

It is a legal requirement that businesses with 5 or more staff formally record their significant findings. It is important to implement the controls that have been identified, ensure staff are trained in new procedures and to check that they are being followed correctly.

Review and Update Risk Assessments

Reviews should take place when:

- Procedures are revised.
- Workplace layout is reorganised.
- New machinery is installed.
- An accident or near miss occurs.
- The law changes.
- The Task, Individual, Load or Environment *(T.I.L.E.)* changes.

Reviews should also take place on a regular basis *(possibly annually)* to ensure nothing has been missed or to identify new techniques or scientific developments that could be introduced to improve safety.

Control Measures and Reducing the Risk of Harm

Reducing the Risks

Where a manual handling task **cannot be avoided** remember **T. I. L. E.**

You should consider:

T – Task

- How will the task be undertaken?
- Can mechanical lifting aids be used?
- Will it involve stretching, twisting or bending?
- Is the task repetitive?
- Is the task work rate target related?

I – Individual

- Who will undertake the task?
- What is their ability?
- Have they received appropriate training?
- Do they have Personal Protective Equipment such as gloves or safety boots if necessary?

L – Load

- How heavy is it?
- What size and shape is it?
- Where is it's centre of gravity?
- Could the load shift during the move?

E – Environment

- Where will the task take place?
- Is there enough space for the manoeuvre?
- Are there any obstacles or hazards?
- Can the layout, lighting or flooring be made safer?

The risk of injury can be reduced by:

- Using mechanical lifting aids wherever possible.
- Planning a resting stage or allowing time between loads so the muscles can recover.
- Avoiding situations where unsafe handling techniques may be used.
- Alternating tasks so individuals don't become bored, lack concentration and make themselves more susceptible to harm.
- Making work rate targets achievable to prevent individuals rushing and compromising their own safety.

- Individuals asking for help and guidance if they feel a manual handling task is beyond their capabilities.
- Attempting to only move loads that are within the physical capability of the individual *(especially if they are pregnant, have a health problem, injury or disability)*.
- Using more than one person if the load is too heavy or large. Good communication between the team is essential.
- Ensuring the correct clothing is worn *(not too tight, with appropriate footwear)*.

- Reducing the load by breaking it down into smaller components.
- Making loads easier to hold by adding handles, insulating hot containers or wearing gloves.
- Not allowing the load to obstruct your view.
- Removing any unnecessary packaging.

- Checking the route is clear and any clutter is removed.
- Checking there is space to put the load down at the final destination.
- Thinking about where heavy or frequently used items are stored.
- Avoiding uneven or slippery floors.
- Making sure the working environment is well lit.

Principles of Safer Handling

Once you have established that the manual handling task cannot be avoided and you have assessed the task and minimised the risks, you need then to follow the correct procedures for completing the task safely.

Testing if a Load is Safe to Lift

Before you even attempt to lift a load, you should always assess whether the load is safe to lift. You can do this by trying to slide the load from side to side with your fingers to see if it moves easily or not. If the load is too awkward in shape or you think it may be too heavy – **GET HELP!** You could also assess if the load could be broken down into smaller pieces to make it easier and safer to lift. If the load is sharp or excessively hot or cold, you will also require personal protective equipment such as gloves or an apron.

Lifting and Returning Loads to a Low Level

Using the following techniques when lifting and lowering objects will make each stage of the task safer.

Feet Positioning

Plan	• Stop and think about the task. • Use T.I.L.E. to assess and reduce the risks as much as possible.
Position	• Get as close to the load as possible. • Position the feet shoulder width apart with the leading leg slightly forward. • If the load has an uneven centre of gravity, position yourself so that the heaviest side is closest to your body.
Lift	• Keep your head up and your shoulders level. • Bend with your knees not your back. • Ensure the load is kept as close to your body as possible, ideally with your elbows at right angles. • Check you have a good grip using your whole hand and not just your fingertips. • Use your leg muscles to smoothly bring the load to waist height.
Move	• Continue to keep the load close to your body. • Avoid twisting and sudden jerky movements. • Make sure you can see where you are going. • Keep carrying distance to a minimum.
Lower	• Use the same principles used for lifting, with the movement reversed to smoothly lower the load. • Take care to avoid crush injuries to fingers and toes when putting the load down.

Note: If carrying more than one object, try to balance the load by carrying equal weight in each hand, e.g. when carrying 2 paint pots, carry one in each hand.

Things to Consider When Lifting and Moving Objects

Pushing Loads

In most cases **pushing a load is preferable to pulling** a load. Before you begin the manoeuvre, ensure the equipment being used is in correct working order, runs smoothly and is suitable for the task. The handles on the equipment should be between waist and shoulder height of the operator. Make sure there is enough friction between the floor and the operator's shoes.

To push the load safely you need to:

- Bend your arms at the elbow and stretch them out to about half their length. This allows you to change the effort required by flexing and extending your arms.
- Keep your hands where they will not get trapped against doors and walls.
- Stand with one foot in front of the other.
- Use your legs and the weight of your body to move the load.
- Tighten your stomach muscles.
- Bend your knees, maintain your spinal curves and lean into the push.
- Keep your feet away from the load and maintain a walking pace.

Pushing up a slope

Negotiating ramps and slopes may require help from another person. The force required to push a load up a slope is considerably more than on a flat surface. The force required to push a load on a flat surface is 2% of the load, e.g. a 400kg load requires an 8kg force to move it. However, on a 1 in 12 *(about 5°)* slope, it would take a 30kg force to push a 400kg load. This is above the guideline weights for both men and women!

If you need to change direction during a push manoeuvre – **DO NOT TWIST!** Always use your feet to change direction.

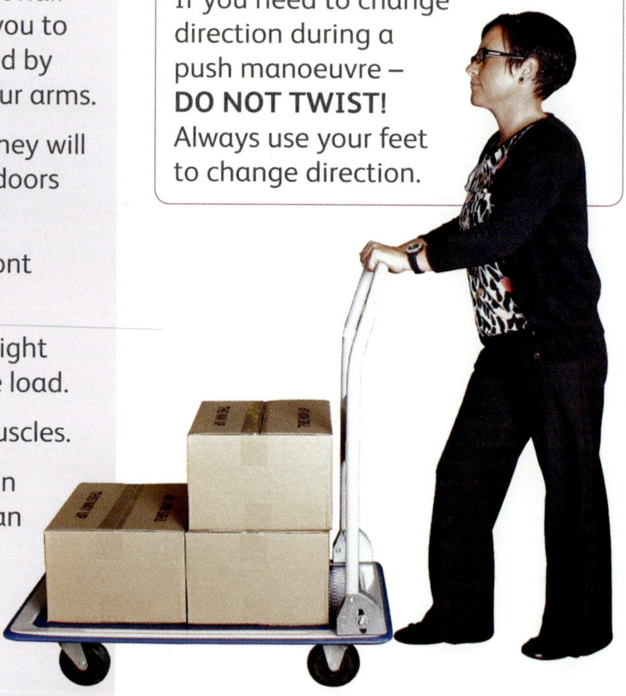

Pulling Loads

Before you begin the manoeuvre, ask yourself if the task could be done more safely by pushing rather than pulling the load. Ensure that the equipment being used is in correct working order, runs smoothly and is suitable for the task. The handles on the equipment should be between waist and shoulder height of the operator. Make sure there is enough friction between the floor and the operator's shoes.

To pull a load safely you need to:

- Keep your hands where they will not get trapped against doors and walls.
- Put one leg behind the other to provide a secure base.
- Maintain your spinal curves and keep your arms as close to your body's centre line as possible.
- Be visually aware of your surroundings as you are not looking in the direction you are going.
- Use your legs and the weight of your body to move the load.
- Keep your feet away from the load and keep to a walking pace.

If you need to change direction during a pull manoeuvre – **DO NOT TWIST!** Always use your feet to change direction.

Team Handling

A load can be shared between individuals to reduce the weight. This means a load may be managed comfortably between a team, where it couldn't be managed by one person alone. However, lifting in a team does not mean that the weight of the object can be doubled by the addition of another person. The capability of a two-person team is approximately two thirds the sum of their individual capacity and a three person team is half the sum of their individual capacity.

Where possible, those lifting should be the same height and build.

Make sure you have assessed and planned the move carefully. In particular make sure you know where you are taking the load, have checked the path is clear from obstruction, that there is space available to put the load down at the final destination and that the load and all team members will fit down the pathway chosen.

To work safely in a team you need to:

- Check there is enough space for the whole team to manoeuvre.
- Check there are enough hand holds for each member of the team.
- Nominate a member of the team to co-ordinate instructions.
- Make sure there is clear communication between team members *(consider effects of noise pollution when working in noisy environments – can everyone hear the instructions?)*.
- Be given clear instruction such as "Ready, Steady, Move" from the nominated person.
- Bend your knees and straighten your legs in unison to keep the load balanced.
- Make sure all members of the team look ahead to maintain their own spinal curves.
- Position your body to avoid twisting.
- Walk in small steps in unison and maintain an appropriate speed of travel – do not rush.

If the load requires a member of the team to walk backwards, this person should not be the team leader. The team leader should always be facing forwards and should communicate clearly with the rest of the team so that nobody has to twist and look over their shoulder to see where they are going.

If you must turn whilst carrying the load – **DO NOT TWIST!** Under instruction from the nominated leader, turn in unison using your feet and not your torso.

Nominated person to give an agreed, clear instruction such as:
"Ready, Steady, Move."

Awkward and Asymmetrical Objects

When lifting and handling asymmetrical or awkward shaped objects, many of the same principals as handling normal shaped loads apply. The main difference is the positioning of your hands on the load. When handling asymmetrical objects you should take hold of the opposite top and bottom corner of the load. If loads are too cumbersome for one person to handle, or you cannot see over the load, you should always seek help.

Working at Low Levels

If the height of the surface you are working on is at a low level and requires you to crouch down, it is far better to kneel than to bend and stoop to complete your task. If working at low levels for extended periods of time change your position regularly.

Lowering From a Height

Lifting from above your shoulder and reaching for loads away from your body puts a strain on your back and arms. Therefore if possible:

- Avoid lifting heavy objects from a height by storing them on a lower shelf in the first place.
- Use a firmly placed stool or stepladder to get closer to the object.
- Slide the object towards you and grip it securely with the whole hand and not just the fingertips.
- Reduce the weight of the object to be lifted by removing some of the contents if necessary.

Manual Handling Equipment

There is a huge range of equipment available designed to be used for manual handling tasks. Getting the right equipment for the task and using it safely is vital. You should always check equipment visually before each use.

Low loader trolleys/platform trolleys

Advantages

- Takes larger loads.
- Handles at waist height for pushing and pulling.

Disadvantages

- Load shelf is low so items require low level lifting.

Considerations

- Wheel size – larger wheels are easier to push.
- Castors improve manoeuvrability.
- Tyres are more suitable for outdoors than solid wheels.
- Is there a need for brakes? Can they be locked?
- A hydraulic platform would prevent stooping.

High loader trolleys

Advantages

- Easy to load and unload without bending.

Disadvantages

- Only suitable for smaller loads.

Considerations

- Handles should be at waist height.
- How secure is the load on the trolley?
- Wheel size – larger wheels are easier to push.
- Castors improve manoeuvrability.
- Tyres are more suitable for outdoors than solid wheels.
- Is there a need for brakes? Can they be locked?

Mechanical lifts e.g. fork lift trucks

Advantages

- Suitable for larger loads.
- Can lift from a height.

Disadvantages

- Requires lots of space to manoeuvre.
- Many other health and safety issues to consider.

Considerations

- Specific training required.
- Effects of vibration from the truck on the operator.
- Noise pollution.

Conveyor belts/roller tracks

Advantages

- Reduces the need to carry loads long distances.

Disadvantages

- Destination of the load is dictated by where the track is set up.
- Risk of entanglement and entrapment in moving mechanical machinery.

Considerations

- All operators need to be fully aware of the health and safety issues when using conveyor belts.
- All hair should be tied back and clothing should not be hanging loose.
- Noise pollution.

Step ladders

Advantages

- Safer than over reaching for items.
- Built for purpose.

Disadvantages

- Involves working at height on a small surface area.
- Can be unstable.

Considerations

- Need to be used on flat even surfaces.
- Handles on the side of the steps can help.
- Steps with a wider base will be more stable.
- Straps are available to attach steps to surrounding structures.
- Help stabilising the ladder may be required.
- People who regularly use ladders may require specific training in this area.

Small ladders/steps e.g. elephant stool

Advantages

- Small and portable.

Disadvantages

- Only raises the user up a small distance.

Considerations

- Need to be used on flat, even surfaces.
- Usually have a weight restriction of approximately 16 stone, so may not be suitable for all members of staff.

Slide sheets

Advantages

- A friction free surface on which to push or pull items.
- Can push and pull with less effort.

Disadvantages

- May make the load unstable.

Considerations

- Distance needed to push and pull – may only be suitable for short distances.
- May restrict the weight of the load you can move.

Mechanical hoists

Advantages

- Can lift heavier loads with minimum effort.
- Decreases the number of staff needed to lift/move a load.

Disadvantages

- Risk of entanglement and entrapment in moving mechanical machinery.
- Hoists can be large which can restrict where they can be used.

Considerations

- Specific training required.
- Lifting equipment should be marked with safe working loads.
- Suitable and stable for use?
- Needs to be positioned and installed to minimise risks *(from loads falling etc)*.
- Require servicing.
- Noise pollution.

Pallet trucks (electric and manual)

Advantages

- Less strenuous moving loads.
- Saves time and needs less manpower.

Disadvantages

- Needs space to manoeuvre.
- Takes up storage space when not in use.

Considerations

- Specific training required.
- Lifting equipment should be marked with safe working loads.
- Suitable and stable for use?
- Requires servicing, lubrication and batteries.
- Effects of vibration from the truck on the operator.
- Noise pollution.

Door openers/magnetic door holds

Advantages

- Once opened, they hold the door open for a length of time.
- Eliminates the need to try and open a door whilst carrying a load.

Considerations

- Holds on fire doors will need to release automatically when the fire alarm sounds.
- Have doors that push open if regularly manual handling through doors e.g. carrying dishes from a kitchen to the restaurant.

Requirements For Testing and Servicing Manual Handling Equipment

Under the requirements of the **Provision and Use of Work Equipment Regulations *(PUWER 1998)***, it is the employer's responsibility to ensure that work equipment is maintained in efficient working order and is suitable for the task. Where any machinery in use has a maintenance log, they must ensure that the log is kept up to date. If the equipment is used in conditions that may cause deterioration, the equipment should be inspected at suitable intervals.

Requirements For Testing and Servicing Lifting Equipment

Lifting equipment has it's own set of regulations – **Lifting Operations and Lifting Equipment Regulations *(LOLER 1998)***. In the case of lifting equipment, an initial thorough examination should be carried out before it is supplied and a further thorough examination should be carried out at least annually. The inspection schedule should be detailed in a written scheme and completed by a 'competent person'. Where lifting equipment is used to lift people, it should be thoroughly inspected every six months. The lifting equipment should be clearly marked with information on safe working loads.

Safe Storage of Manual Handling Equipment

When not in use, manual handling equipment should be stored safely to avoid the risk of obstruction and people tripping or falling over it. Where possible, avoid storing manual handling equipment in conditions that could cause the equipment to deteriorate e.g. storing outside where rain could rust the wheels on a trolley.

Test Your Knowledge

1. **What is the safest position in which to carry a load?** *Page 22*
   A. Close to the floor.
   B. Close to your body.
   C. At arms length.
   D. Over your shoulder.

2. **What does T.I.L.E. stand for in risk assessment?** *Page 20*
   A. Team, Individual, Leader, Execute.
   B. Tilt, Incline, Lean, Enable.
   C. Task, Individual, Load, Environment.
   D. Tools, Industry, Levers, Engage.

3. **What is it most important to do when lifting as a team?** *Page 26*
   A. Work in friendship groups.
   B. Take turns holding the heavy end.
   C. Have good hygiene procedures.
   D. Appoint a leader and communicate well.

4. **According to Health and Safety Laws, what should employees make their employer aware of?** *Page 6*
   A. Feeling undervalued.
   B. Dangers in the workplace.
   C. New technology.
   D. Unauthorised absences.

5. **When risk assessing a load which of the following aspects is the most important?** *Page 18*
   A. Value.
   B. Weight.
   C. Colour.
   D. Branding.

Glossary

Accident
An unplanned or unexpected event which causes damage to persons, equipment, stock, buildings etc.

Accident Book
Forms on which details of all accidents may be recorded.

Acute
An effect on the body that occurs rapidly after a short exposure to a health hazard.

Arthritis
Inflammation of a joint that can be caused by wear and tear due to repetitive tasks.

Breach
The infringement of a legal right or duty.

Cartilage
Firm rubbery tissue that cushions bones at the joints and allows for smooth movement.

Centre of Gravity
The point at which the whole weight of an object can be considered to act and therefore at which all parts of an object are balanced.

Chronic
An effect on the body that occurs after a long period of exposure or repeated exposure to a health hazard.

Competent Person
A person who has sufficient training, experience, knowledge or other relevant qualities to enable them to undertake a task/job.

Control Measure
Actions or procedures put in place to reduce risk to an acceptable level.

Discs
A disc shaped piece of specialised tissue that separate the vertebral bones of the spinal column. They enable the spine to flex and extend, allow smooth movement of the spine and help bond the vertebrae together.

Ergonomics
The application of science information concerning human beings and the design of objects, systems and environments for human use.

Force
A push or pull on an object resulting from two objects interacting with each other.

Fracture
A break in bone or cartilage.

Fulcrum
The point or support on which a lever rests or pivots.

Hazard
Something that has the potential to cause harm.

Hernia
A protrusion of tissue through a weakness in the muscle or surrounding tissue wall.

Hierarchy of Control
Control Measures listed in order of priority.

HSE
Health and Safety Executive. Non-departmental public body responsible for workplace health, safety and welfare.

Liability
Legal obligation or duty.

Ligaments

Band of fibrous tissue connecting bones or cartilage. Can hold joints together.

Load
An object to be moved held or positioned.

Manual Handling
Using physical effort to lift, carry, push or pull a load.

Musculoskeletal Disorders
Injury to the musculoskeletal system including problems such as lower back pain, joint injuries and repetitive strain injuries of various sorts.

Musculoskeletal System
The system in the body of bones, muscles, ligaments and tendons.

Nucleus
Inner gelatine-like core of the discs.

Occupational Health
The promotion and maintenance of physical and mental well being of all staff.

PPE
Personal Protective Equipment or equipment worn to protect the wearer against hazards.

Reasonably Practicable
A risk/sacrifice computation made to see what safety measures are reasonable under given circumstances of cost/benefit.

Risk
The likelihood of the hazard actually doing damage.

Risk Assessment
A proactive technique for preventing accidents and illness by identifying problems and introducing control measures.

Slipped Disc
When the layers of cartilage of the disc become cracked and the inner nucleus pushes out of the crack and presses on the spinal nerve.

Spinal Cord
The major column of nerve tissue that is connected to the brain and lies within the vertebral canal.

Spinal Nerves
Nerves that originate in the spinal cord. There are 31 pairs of spinal nerves.

Sprain or Strain
The muscle or ligament fibres tear as a result of overstretching.

Stability
The ability of an object to return to a balanced position with the same base of support after being disturbed.

Static Work
Any posture held for longer than 30 seconds.

Suitable and Sufficient
Decide if the risk assessment is appropriate for the given circumstances. Is it detailed enough with regard to the level of risk involved?

Tendons
Fibrous band of connective tissue by which muscles attach to bones.

Vertebrae
Plural of vertebra. A vertebra is one of the 33 bony segments that form the spinal column of humans.

Vibration
Continuous quick, slight shaking movement.

Young Person
A person who has ceased to be a child *(over school leaving age)* but is not yet 18.

Notes

Notes

Notes